MIX
Papier aus verantwortungsvollen Quellen
Paper from responsible sources
FSC® C105338

Tatjana Kennedy

Anglicism Usage in German Political Language

The German Greens' Election Manifesto

Anchor Compact

Kennedy, Tatjana: Anglicism Usage in German Political Language: The German
Greens' Election Manifesto. Hamburg, Anchor Academic Publishing 2014

Buch-ISBN: 978-3-95489-208-2
PDF-eBook-ISBN: 978-3-95489-708-7
Druck/Herstellung: Anchor Academic Publishing, Hamburg, 2014

Bibliografische Information der Deutschen Nationalbibliothek:
Die Deutsche Nationalbibliothek verzeichnet diese Publikation in der Deutschen
Nationalbibliografie; detaillierte bibliografische Daten sind im Internet über
http://dnb.d-nb.de abrufbar

Bibliographical Information of the German National Library:
The German National Library lists this publication in the German National Bibliography.
Detailed bibliographic data can be found at: http://dnb.d-nb.de

All rights reserved. This publication may not be reproduced, stored in a retrieval system
or transmitted, in any form or by any means, electronic, mechanical, photocopying,
recording or otherwise, without the prior permission of the publishers.

Das Werk einschließlich aller seiner Teile ist urheberrechtlich geschützt. Jede Verwertung
außerhalb der Grenzen des Urheberrechtsgesetzes ist ohne Zustimmung des Verlages
unzulässig und strafbar. Dies gilt insbesondere für Vervielfältigungen, Übersetzungen,
Mikroverfilmungen und die Einspeicherung und Bearbeitung in elektronischen Systemen.

Die Wiedergabe von Gebrauchsnamen, Handelsnamen, Warenbezeichnungen usw. in
diesem Werk berechtigt auch ohne besondere Kennzeichnung nicht zu der Annahme,
dass solche Namen im Sinne der Warenzeichen- und Markenschutz-Gesetzgebung als frei
zu betrachten wären und daher von jedermann benutzt werden dürften.

Die Informationen in diesem Werk wurden mit Sorgfalt erarbeitet. Dennoch können
Fehler nicht vollständig ausgeschlossen werden und die Diplomica Verlag GmbH, die
Autoren oder Übersetzer übernehmen keine juristische Verantwortung oder irgendeine
Haftung für evtl. verbliebene fehlerhafte Angaben und deren Folgen.

Alle Rechte vorbehalten

© Anchor Academic Publishing, ein Imprint der Diplomica® Verlag GmbH
http://www.diplom.de, Hamburg 2014
Printed in Germany

List of Contents

1. INTRODUCTION 7

2. THEORETICAL FRAMEWORK 10
    2.1. THE GERMAN GREEN PARTY: IDEOLOGY, TARGET GROUP AND COMMUNICATION TECHNIQUES 10
    2.2. DISCOURSE ANALYSIS: POLITICAL RHETORIC 13
    2.3. CONTACT LINGUISTICS 14
        2.3.1. The Historical Background of English and German Language Contact 14
        2.3.2. English and German Identities 16
        2.3.3. English: Source Language, Transfer and Dominance 17
        2.3.4. Classification of Contact-induced outcomes: Code-switching or Borrowing? 18
        2.3.5. Classification of Contact- induced outcomes: What is an Anglicism? 19
        2.3.6. Method and Classification Terminology of Analysis 20

3. EMPIRICAL ANALYSIS OF "DER GRÜNE NEUE GESELLSCHAFTSVERTRAG" 22
        3.1.1. The Framework 22
        3.1.2. Rhetorical Devices: Parallelisms, Metaphors and 'the rule of three' 23
        3.1.3. Presuppositions 25
    3.2. ANGLICISMS WITHIN THE GREEN'S LANGUAGE 26
        3.2.1. Levels of text composition. Location, Order and Frequency of Anglicisms 26
        3.2.2. Lexical level: Borrowings, Hybrids and Pseudo- Anglicisms 27

4. A GREEN LANGUAGE? 32

5. SUMMARY AND CONCLUSION 36

6. BIBLIOGRAPHY 39

1. Introduction

Every four years on Election Day, German citizens make their way to the ballot boxes to vote for the political party and candidate they would favour entering the government. These voters however, might not be aware of the fact that whether their choice has resulted from political conviction or not, the set of political attitudes which has found their favour has been the result of a complex communication strategy the individual party carried out long beforehand. As Loscher states: "[...] language is one of the most obvious means through which power is exercised" (2004: 34).

Election manifestos [1] that are published months before the actual Election Day represent a political campaign. This campaign's ideology is embedded in a certain kind of language which will persuade and satisfy the readers. These readers are either potential voters that need to be enthused or core voters that have to be pleased so as to vote 'their' party again, relying on a recognition value in the manifesto. Professional speechwriters and advertising agencies accentuate political election manifestos in a way so that the visual aspect, the text components and the choice of phrases represent the 'style' of a text (cf. Harms 2008: 16). This style has to convey a coherent message, which represents the party as a whole and makes out the communicative framework. To add more impact, these speechwriters include persuasive language, insert rhetorical devices, and integrate 'modern' words such as anglicisms.

So by studying the language of a political party, and taking two different linguistic fields into consideration – here discourse linguistics and contact linguistics – it becomes apparent how perceptions and ideas of people and, subsequently, political convictions are influenced by language. In this study, the focus will be put on the specific language used by the German Green Party (BÜNDNIS90/DIE GRÜNEN) in its 224 pages strong manifesto of 2009 which the party published in May 2009. This manifesto provided the basis for its public campaign in the context of the elections for the Bundestag in the same year.

---

[1] 'Election manifesto', the English translation for 'Wahlprogramm' will serve as main reference term for 'election program'.

The aim of this study is to linguistically analyse the language of the German Green party's language in order to find out whether such a thing as a "green language" exists.

Background, Material and Method

In the year of 2009, the German Green Party had just experienced an immense gain of attention through the rising influence of ecological issues in politics. The increasing media-attention for an emotionally charged field of topics, subsumed under the slogan: "Save the Planet", lead to different results. On the one hand newly constituted green parties emerged all over the world, and on the other hand, the already existing green parties gained a great deal of attention. Not only in European societies but also, among others, in the U.S., green issues became relevant. Here, Barack Obama built up a "green team" to enforce his energy and environmental agenda, thus being the first American president since the days of the Carter government in the 1970s, to give a serious concern to these topics.

In Germany, the Greens as *the* party to be concerned with environmental protection issues, presented in their political manifesto of 2009 a very broad scope of topics. These topics represented a group within Germany's society where the political concept of being 'green' involved a consciousness towards a healthy dealing with nature, respect for equal rights (women's rights, equal civil rights for gays and lesbians, et cetera) and the support of policies on sustainable production and consumption and renewable energies.

The target group responding to these 'green concepts' has long grown from a rather small group into a large mass in which these concepts are conceived as an established set of ideological principles. The Green Party had therefore left the position of an outsider within the group of parties in Germany's political landscape and, in 2009, resembled an established party addressing 'Zeitgeist' issues. These issues were simultaneously also being taken up by other German parties such as the SPD and DIE LINKE denoting a certain 'trend' of 'green topics'.

There are two decisive questions arising from this situation: Does the Green party create an own 'green language' to transmit its program that is do the words which have been in the limelight of this study suggest that they belong to a canon of words bearing green connotations which are strongly related to a "green" discourse? Or does the Green party rather use certain words that exist anyway, also beyond the 'green' speech community?

The method to find an answer to these questions will be stated in the following.

In a first step, the study is divided into two parts. The first part presents a theoretical approach and is conducted to give a general insight into the different discursive processes and the contact linguistic traits of a political speech or text. Hereby the terminology and a classification of the topics relevant for the research question will be announced.

The second part will present the empirical analysis of the Green party's manifesto, examine certain metaphorical expressions with regards to their form and meaning and analyse English borrowings, hybrids and pseudo loans on contact linguistic level. This empirical part will be completed by a summary of the previous findings in respect to their implicational value.

Since the issues of political language, language change and especially anglicisms present a broad and complex array of approaches and different fields of discourse, the study has to disregard a few topics to limit its extent.

To keep up a coherent and cohesive structure, many of the German citations have not been translated, also bearing in mind that the readers of this work will have no problem in understanding both languages.

2. Theoretical Framework

In the beginning of the following theoretical part, the Green Party will be examined. Here, a focus will be but on answering questions on the ideology behind the "Green" concept as well as on the type and structure of both its target group and its techniques of communication, especially within its state election programs. With this immersion into the 'world' of the Green party it will be shown for which purpose the party communicates, to whom and how it usually presents its ideology in order to get a comprehensive insight that will help analysing the Greens language in a later chapter.

2.1. The German Green Party: Ideology, Target Group and Communication Techniques

The Party's Ideology

The German Green Party announced its first basic program in 1980. In this set of principles, the essential values and aims of the Green party were established. Even though the party has gone through many internal and external-induced changes, those fundamentals are still visible in its policies today. Erik Harms (2008) summarizes the Green ideology in the beginning of his paper "Der kommunikative Stil der Grünen im historischen Wandel". He refers to the Green manifesto of 1980 and states:

> Sie verstehen sich als eine systemkritische Bewegungspartei, die eine rasche Umstrukturierung der Gesamtgesellschaft nach den Vorgaben des postmaterialistischen Wertekanon anstrebt, eine auf Kompromisse ausgerichtete Kooperation mit den traditionellen Parlamentsparteien kategorisch ablehnt, [...], und für eine Stärkung der dezentralen, direkten Demokratie eintritt (vgl. Die Grünen 1980, 4f) (Harms 2008:9)

Obviously this strong all-or-nothing approach has been modified since and adapted to an attitude that fits the party`s role as a "parliament party of the traditional kind" (Harms 2008: 10). This is the part they play in German politics today. Currently the Greens hold 68 seats (of 622) within the German Federal Parliament (*Bundestag*) which results from their election result of a total of 10, 7% of the votes in the parliament elections of 2009[2].

---

[2] (cf. http://www.bundestag.de/btg_wahl/index.html.)

Since their first election for Parliament in 1980 this has been the party's best result ever. After leaping from 1,5% in the 1980 Bundestag election up to 8,3% in 1987, the Greens' outcome stayed relatively constant, ranging between approximately 7 and 8 per cent. The rise from 8,1% in the Bundestag elections in 2005 up to the 10,7% in the election of 2009 can be explained by different influential factors, such as the growing influence of energy and climate-change policies but also by the green party's communication and language.

According to Harms (2008), the success of a political program based on an important principle of success that he calls, with reference to Josef Klein, the "Kommunikationsmaxime" (Harms 2008: 12). This maxim summons the party to be cautious of the way in which to communicate their election program (cf. 2008:12) by way of the order: "Mache dir durch dein Bundestagswahlprogramm möglichst wenig Gegner in der relevanten Wählergruppe" (2008:12).

The order's implications are important. Harms (2008:12) argues that this principle pressures the political party – as the text producer – first to intensely analyse their text recipient. This means that the party has first to identify, then focus on one target group and anticipate the expectations this target group has in regards to the text content of the program (cf. Harms: 2008:12).

The Party's Target Group

One main factor behind texting a manifesto is choosing the language with an eye towards the language's intelligibility. Whatever stylistic reasoning behind the choice of language – it is of utter importance that the readers can understand the words and grasp the message. Thus, the language of a manifesto and its target audience are closely connected.

The following citation was extracted from a published university research paper that was conducted to analyse the Green's previous election campaign of 2005. Even though dating four years back in time, it still draws a picture of what the target group might have looked like in the relevant election campaign of 2009.

> Aufgrund der Parteigeschichte und überzeugung sprechen Bündnis 90/Die Grünen eine bestimmte Klientel an Wählern an. Vor allem <u>junge, gut gebildete Wähler</u>, die eine finanziell gesicherte Existenz aufweisen, zählen zur Wählerschaft der Partei. (Dietrich/Keim 2006:8[3]) [emphasis added].

---

[3] (cf. http://www.fb9dv.uni-duisburg.de/wis/WIS5/Gruene/Medienarchiv/GrueneKampage.pdf.)

Of special importance are the adjunctions 'young' and 'well educated' with regards to the Green voters. These young and well-educated Germans make up a certain speech community that has its own canon of words and discourses that is of interest. When aiming at bonding with this group, not only the topics but also the language has to associate with it. How the Greens manage to do so will be looked at in the following.

The Communication Techniques of the Greens

Corresponding to their voter profile, the Green Party has long been in favour of words or phrases which contain rhetorical devices and English origins. Manfred Görlach's "More Englishes" shows an election poster of the Green Party from 1986 where a combination of an anglicism together with the technique of persuasive language is used to convey a political message. Görlach (2005: 86) shows the poster on which it says: "Smogging? Die Alternative ist Grün".

Firstly, we are confronted with the *anglicism* 'smogging' which in itself is a blend of Smog (that, again, combines 'smoke and Fog') and Jogging" (2005: 86). Secondly, a *presupposition* is applied, implying the viewers know what jogging and smog is. The definition of anglicisms and presuppositions will follow in the next chapter.

In terms of the Green election campaign's communication, this study focuses on the Bundestag election of 2009 in which the advertising agency "Zum goldenen Hirschen" stood as creative brain behind most of the communication and visual strategies of the Greens. They have been the party`s direct marketers and advertisers since the national elections in 2002 and call themselves 'close' to the Green party. In a public statement on the Green Party's member magazine website, it says that the ad agency aimed at providing the Green Party with a "modern and unusual" campaign.

Julian Scholl, executive director at "Zum Goldenen Hirschen" says:

> Wir wollen auffallen durch einen zeitgemäßen Wahlkampf, eine moderne Sprache und ungewöhnliche Aktionen. Der Wahlkampf wird auch an Orten stattfinden, wo man die Grünen sonst eher nicht erwartet.[4] [emphasis added]

---

[4] (cf. http://www.gruene-partei.de/cms/themen_mitgliederzeitschrift/dok/1/1322.vorgestellt.htm)

The announcement that the Greens want to receive attention not only by means of a modern campaign but also through 'modern' language, serves as a point of analysis that will be discussed later on.

2.2. Discourse analysis: Political Rhetoric

In this chapter some expressions or sentences that stuck out whilst reading the Greens manifesto will be outlined, in order get an overview on the strategies the Greens used to influence, convince, confirm or appeal to their readership.

Beard (2000) argues that just like any other field of social activity, also the sphere of politics has an own language variety, a 'code' (Beard 2000: 5). Such a code consists of certain terms and is also constructed by the use of rhetorical devices. The reason behind the use of this code is to win the voters. "One of the goals of politicians must be to persuade their audience of the validity of their basic claims." (Jones/Stillwell Peccei 2004: 42).

"Metaphors, Parallelisms, or the 'rule of three'" (Jones/Stillwell Peccei 2004: 49) are means for politicians to rhetorically "increase the impact of their ideas" (Jones/Stillwell Peccei 2004: 45) and by that to convince the reader of these thoughts with the aim to receive his or her vote. The Green Party uses all of these three rhetorical devices, and many more, extensively within their program. Examples of each rhetorical device will make apparent how they work and will also serve as an introduction to the Green style of language within the program.

Amongst all of the tools that exist in political speech, Jones and Stilwell Peccei present the reader also with 'presupposition' and 'implicature' (cf. Jones/Stillwell Peccei 2004: 42). Presuppositions are "background assumptions" (2004: 42) that hide behind sentences or phrases, and that are "taken for granted to be true regardless of whether the whole sentence is true". (2004: 42).

Jones and Stilwell Peccei (2004: 42) moreover mention four different ways in which a presupposition can enter a sentence. That is a) through adjectives, and in most cases through adjectives that have a comparative character. b) through possessives, like apostrophe -s possessives in English or the "Possesivpronomen" in German; c) by way of subordinate clauses; and d) by using questions instead of statements.

2.3. Contact linguistics

For any investigation into the language of a certain group it's important to take into consideration the issues of the language's etymology and its current position in the world of languages. Thus, the following theoretical chapter is divided up into three consecutive subchapters. Firstly a historical background to the contact of English and German is given, secondly a brief insight into the role of English in this contact situation and finally a classification is made, regarding the contact-induced outcomes; namely anglicisms. This is done to show what different linguistic methods the Greens used to transport their ideology.

2.3.1. The Historical Background of English and German Language Contact

In this part the essay aligns itself with Busse and Görlach (2004: 13).

In their chapter on language contact history, Busse and Görlach state that the cultural exchange between the two nations of Britain and Germany can be traced back to the fifth century, when the British isles were inhabited by the North German and Southern Danish settlers. Later on, the transfer of English borrowings into German was "infrequent and restricted to certain domains" (Busse/Görlach 2002: 13). The authors provide the reader with a historical timeline of English and German language contact. In six steps, they describe the language contact from the British influence in the eighteenth century via literature, architecture, sciences and so on up to the 1990's when globalization reached a new peak. The widespread use of media was intensified with the arrival of new technologies such as the World Wide Web which enabled an increasing influence of the American culture on Germany (cf. Busse/Görlach 2002: 13f.).

As a fairly early result of this language intrusion, an opposing attitude established itself within Germany. Already in the eighteenth century "allergic reactions" (Busse/Görlach 2002: 13) towards lexical borrowings appeared, aimed at the French influence that in its peak phase almost replaces German as a "[…] *spoken* means of communication among the well-to-do and educated."(cf. Busse/Görlach 2002: 15f.).

The second uproar against foreign linguistic influence was directed against English. The 'Allgemeiner Deutscher Sprachverein' was founded in 1885, speaking out against English words in the German lexicon. Later this opposition against

English specialized its critique against borrowings from the field of sport which had risen in importance around 1900. A resistance going beyond borrowings came with the Nazi regime in the 1930's. Their revolt was directed not only against English borrowings, but also against the American lifestyle, claiming the liberal thought was "particularly dangerous to the German psyche" (Görlach/Busse 2002:17).

An interesting fact, however, is that the Nazi's "witchhunt of foreignisms" (Polenz cit. in Görlach/Busse 2002: 17) ended when Nazi leaders noticed the strength of foreign words for the use of propaganda (cf. Busse/ Görlach 2003: 16/17). The knowledge and usage of foreign words in political discourse is therefore nothing new in German political speech.

In the following, a brief insight on the development of English, regardless of its contact on German will serve as essential background information for the preceding chapter. When looking at the change of influence of English, Braj B. Kachru, Jubilee Professor Emeritus at the University Illinois, stands as a distinguished expert in this field and his circular model presenting 'English as a World language' has become a foundation for the work of many linguists.. In Kachru's circular model of "World Englishes" from 1985, Great Britain, the U.S., Canada, Australia and New Zealand make up "the first circle". They present the varieties of English that serve as source languages for the languages in the embracing circles and are therefore called "Spendersprachvarietäten" (Knospe 2010). The next, and second circle assembles the colonial states in Africa or Asia that were once conquered by the British Empire where the once established English varieties now experiences new structures, differentiating themselves from the first circle English variety (cf. Knospe 2010).

The main interest in respect to this work lies in the third, the "expanding circle" (Bolton/Kachru 2006: 7) of English varieties. English in Europe or "European English" (Bolton/Kachru 2006: 10) is the currently dominating language of culture and can take over the function of an integrating, instrumentally second language:

> Als aktuell dominierende Kultursprache kann das Englische dort die Funktion einer integrierenden, instrumentellen Zweitsprache übernehmen (Koll-Stobbe cit. in Knospe 2010).

The influence of English in Europe has thus clearly risen from its restricted EFL Status (English as a foreign language) which had only the aim to serve for "[...] scholarly, commercial, technological, and diplomatic purposes" (Görlach 1995: 7).

This expanding role of English in Europe is also described by Jennifer Jenkins who marks that:

> [...] English is evolving as a European *lingua franca* not only in restricted fields such as business and commerce, but also in a wide range of other contexts of communication including its increasing use as a language of socialisation. (Jenkins 2003:38).

However, the implications behind this increase of English linguistic influence in Europe are also tied to the increase of the English culture's influence in Europe.

2.3.2. English and German Identities

> Since at least the time of the Ancient Greeks, sholars have argued for a causative link between culture and language (that is a community's cultural experience and resultant worldview 'shapes', in Saussurean terms, their *langue*) [emphasis added] (Jones/Stilwell Peccei 2004: 24).

This argument states that the connection of culture and language has existed long before studies on contact linguistics were conducted. The common denominator that incorporates both culture and language is identity. "Identity is linked with culture as well as with language" (Bolton/ Kachru 2006: 12). This concept of identity plays a major role when analysing the motifs behind contact-induced language change.

The emergence of two cultural identities, namely the German cultural identity and its counterpart; the general English or global/international identity (translated: Koll-Stobbe 2009: 31), is the result of the different and widespread functions that the English language fulfils in German. With reference to Koll-Stobbe (2009: 30), English in Germany has the following functions:

- The language of education,
- The lingua franca of the consumer culture,
- As "*Business English*" a certified qualification in career,
- The language of youth culture
- The language of the entertainment culture (Music, internet, ect.)

But not only the emergence of two separate identities results from these different functional areas of English. Koll-Stobbe also states that when speakers in German are functional bilinguals, they are more apt to switch between the languages as in the code- switching process or simply by borrowing English units:

> [...] funktionale Zweisprachigkeit entwickelt sich eine größere Selbstverständlichkeit, zwischen den Sprachkodes des Deutschen und des Englischen hin- und herzuwechseln." (2009: 30).

Later in the analysis of the essay, a closer look will be put on the topic of code-switching as mentioned by Koll-Stobbe.

2.3.3. English: Source Language, Transfer and Dominance

When two languages "meet", either through an actual contact, an "immediate speaker contact" (Onysko 2000: 44) (in the course of conquests, colonies, e.g.), or through mediated contact, the input of English words in the media for instance, the result is the same. In both contact situations the "[...] vehicles of contact-induced change." (Winford 2007: 26) are called 'borrowing' and 'imposition'[5]. (cf. Winford 2007: 26)

The terminology for the two languages involved in a contact situation is taken over from Winford (2007: 5) and Onysko (2007: 6). In almost every language contact situation there is one **source language** (SL) and one **recipient language** (RL)[6]. The activity between the SL and RL can be regarded as *transfer* of speech components from the one language to another. In what order this transfer happens is stated by Winford:

> The direction of transfer of linguistic features is always from the source language to the RL, and the agent of transfer can be either the recipient language or the source language speaker." (In the former case, we have borrowing (RL agentivity), in the latter, imposition (SL agentivity) (Winford 2007: 26).

So having cleared up the direction of transfer, the question arises, who in the case of English and German resembles the SL, and who the RL. Hereby the topic of **language dominance** comes into action. Winford (2007: 26) refers to Van Coetsem's definition according to which it depends on the fact which one of two languages is active and therefore the 'agent' in this contact situation. If in that matter, the RL is active, it is the RL which is the dominant language and vice versa (cf.

---

[5] In this study however, only the notion of 'borrowing' will be regarded in order to limit the scope.
[6] Alternatively, SL is also called "[...]'donor language', 'substrate', 'replica language' and the like." (Winford 2007: 26).

Van Coetsem cit. in Winford 2007: 26). In the case of English and German, the agent of transfer is German. German speakers borrow English words and are therefore the agent. This makes German to the linguistically dominant language in this contact situation. Onysko supports this dominance theorie. He says that in the process of language contact *borrowing* is the transfer or transmission of linguistic material from a "subdominant SL (English) to dominant RL (German)" (cf. 2007: 44).

2.3.4. Classification of Contact-induced outcomes: Code-switching or Borrowing?

Before any terminology-related entanglements appear, this chapter will try to draw a distinction between the two transfer processes of code switching and borrowing. This is done in order to find a comprehensive insight into the process that lead to the distinct anglicisms the Greens used in their manifesto.

Neither Onysko nor Winford or Görlach, manage to come up with a consistent and clear-cut differentiation between these two contact- induced results. This work will therefore use Koll-Stobbe's (2009: 32f.) classification as a base for the following examinations. In a first step Koll-Stobbe draws a division line between the levels on which both code-switches and borrowings become active. She argues that on the one side code-switches are processes of transfer on discourse level: "sozial, kognitiv oder stilistisch motivierte(n) Transferprozesse, die auf der Ebene interaktiver Diskurse wirksam werden[…]"[…]".(Koll-Stobbe 2009: 32). Borrowings on the other side, are a process on the "[…]Ebene des Lexikons[…]".(Koll-Stobbe 2009: 32). So far, this provides the reader with a two-level approach which helps to arrange the terms. In a next step Koll-Stobbe (2009: 33) then conducts a juxtaposition of both processes' traits in terms of transfer. The results of this comparison are listed below (cf. Koll-Stobbe 2009: 32):

Code- switching:

- The transfer of either one or many word units (lexemes)
- A synchronic process (ad hoc)
- A discursively and interactive process (e.g. happens in dialogues)
- May adapt or integrate single- and multiword units on phonological and morphological level

Borrowing:

- The transfer of lexemes
- A diachronic process (over time)
- The direction of transfer is directed at the language system
- The Transfer function is to extend the lexicon
- May adapt or integrate single- and multiword units on phonological, morphological and semantic level
- Frequently used and expected
- Lexicalized
- Can shift in meaning

The enumeration of the traits in both processes simplifies a differentiation between both. Nevertheless, the subject of analysis is the entry of anglicisms into the German speech. In what different ways anglicisms are able to adapt to the German language, Koll-Stobbe (2009: 36) states in a comprising gesture:

> Anglizismen können sowohl über Prozesse des spontanen Sprachwechsels oder codeswitching, im Sinne eines Wortbildungsmusters "Entlehnung", als auch als Identitätsmerkmale nativisierender Sprachprozesse (hybride Bildungen, Scheinentlehnungen) im Deutschen wirken.

This leads to an important conclusion with regards to the linguistic analysis of the manifesto. A written manifesto is no discourse situation. A manifesto has the quality of a "One-to-Many" type of communication. Therefore no synchronic or spontaneous 'ad-hoc' switching from German to English and back again can occur. Thus, the act of code- switching within the Greens manifesto can be excluded.

The analysis of the "contact-induced language influence" (Heine/Kuteva 2005: 122) of the political manifesto will therefore concentrate on the word formation process "borrowing" and the proofs for language assimilation: hybrids and pseudo loans.

2.3.5. Classification of Contact- induced outcomes: What is an Anglicism?

Onysko says it quite right in his opening chapter that "One of the core issues in the field of language contact is how to classify the linguistic influence that a language (source language SL) exerts on another language (receptor language, RL)" (Onysko 2007:10). The following chapter of this study will tackle this core issue and will try to classify the linguistic influence in that case: anglicisms.

The definition what anglicisms are in the context of this study is lent from Onysko (2007: 90). He breaks down his depiction of an anglicism to the following sentence: [...] An *anglicism* is any instance of an English lexical, structural, and phonological element in German that can be formally related to English."(cf. 2007: 90) He further elaborates his definition by saying that the [...] term *anglicism* includes borrowings, codeswitches, and the productive use of English forms in German (semantic changes, hybrids, and pseudo anglicisms)" (cf. 2007: 90) Moreover also „instances of interference and unobtrusive borrowings" (cf. 2007: 90) are considered to be anglicisms, but this won't be deplored deeper in this work.

2.3.6. Method and Classification Terminology of Analysis

In order to get a picture of what kind of source text we are dealing with, first a look is taken at the exterior structure of the Greens manifesto and secondly at the frequency and appearance of anglicisms. After this surface-structure analysis has been conducted, the deep structure is examined. Here the paper is checked for borrowings, hybrids and pseudo- anglicisms and their semantic implications. The terminology of each language phenomenon will be given in the following:

Borrowings

Onysko (2007: 36) states that borrowing is a process, mostly happening on the level of lexis and that it is assimilated morphologically and in parts phonologically in the receptor language (RL). Next to that, he recites that borrowings are single-word importation that are "paradigmatically incorporated and follow the syntagmatically relations of the RL [...]." (2007:36).

Hybrid Anglicisms

Referring to Onysko's (2007: 55) definition; hybrid anglicisms, or hybrids, are the result of a compounding process of both English borrowings and German word components. The process of derivation, like affixation of "borrowed bases" (cf. 2007:55) and compound productions, leads to "the notion of hybridity" (cf. 2007:55). In all word classes of German hybrids can be found, whereas compound nouns are the most often used hybrids. These compound noun hybrids were also used primarily within the Greens election program and will play a special role in the analysis.

Pseudo- anglicisms

Pseudo-anglicisms (Onysko 2008: 52) or pseudo-loans, as Busse and Görlach call them (Görlach 2002: 29), describe the word formation process in which one lexeme or more lexemes from a source language (here: English), are used to create an expression in the receptor language (here: German) which does not exist in the source language English (cf. Onysko 2008: 52). Busse and Görlach (2002: 29) differentiate between three kinds of pseudo-anglicisms, categorizing them into lexical, morphological and semantic pseudo-loans. Onysko opposes this division by stating that these classifications lead to a "blur(s)" between the categories without drawing a connection to "an English Model" (2007: 52). He says that pseudo- anglicisms such as "Happy End" derive from "English models whose meanings are retained in the German variants" (cf. 2007: 52). Therefore, it is partly wrong to draw a distinct line between morphological and semantic borrowed pseudo- anglicisms.

3. Empirical Analysis of "Der Grüne Neue Gesellschaftsvertrag"

In the following part, the theoretical concept that has served as foundation will be filled with empirical content. In order to dig deeper into the structure of political discourse, first of all an analysis of rhetorical devices is done. To limit the scope of the study, only some prominent phrases and expressions were extracted and analysed: they represent exemplary samples which stand for the text style as a whole. Here the analysis follows Jones and Stillwell Peccei (2002) framework of political language.

In the second part, the anglicisms that were extracted from the political manifesto will be examined on levels of form and meaning. All along the path of analysis, the research question will serve as a guide: *Why* were these words used and do the examined words stand for a "Green" meaning or belong to a "Green" inspired field of language?

3.1.1. The Framework

The „Der Grüne Neue Gesellschaftsvertrag" stretches out over 234 Pages. Its structure is dived up into a title page, a table of contents, a preamble and a main part; consisting of 14 chapters that are topped off by a conclusion. The title page shows next to the headline: 'Der Grüne Neue Gesellschaftsvertrag', also four of the Greens base topics: "Klima, Arbeit, Gerechtigkeit und Freiheit". Beneath these principles the blue tinted outlines of the earth (Eurocentric view) occupy the lower half of the page. In the lower right hand corner, the Greens logo that was last changed in 2007, is positioned.

The 14 chapters of the manifesto have 5 to 30 subchapters that are all subsumed under short and precisely formulated headlines. The topics are: economy, energy, social topics (fair wages, etc), education, equal rights, integration and fair justice, democracy, East & West Germany, equality of Women & Men, culture & creativity, Internet & Europe and social responsibility (freely translated and summarized from the DGNG 2009).

3.1.2. Rhetorical Devices: Parallelisms, Metaphors and 'the rule of three'

Parallelisms

The device of Parallelism is used right in the preamble, the introductory part. Here the part "Es liegt an uns" (Der Grüne Neue Gesellschaftsvertrag (DGNG[7]) 2009:13) is repeated five times so as to "emphasize that the ideas are equal in importance and can add a sense of symmetry and rhythm,[...]" (cf. Jones/ Stilwell Peccei 2004: 51). Beard (2000: 39) adds that "In long speeches word-repetition can be used to hold the speech together, but also to emphasize moral values."

> Es liegt an uns, jetzt die Grundlagen dafür zu legen, dass neue Arbeit geschaffen wird und die Wirtschaft ein Fundament bekommt, das auch in Zukunft trägt. Es liegt an uns, die Welt so einzurichten, dass wir unser Klima schützen, anstatt es zu zerstören. Es liegt an uns, dass wir unsere Gesellschaft gerechter machen und Blockaden wegräumen, die verhindern, dass jede und jeder eine echte Chance auf Teilhabe hat. Es liegt an uns, Bürgerrechte in unserer Gesellschaft zu stärken und sie nicht weiter abzubauen. Und es liegt an uns, dass wir jetzt die Grundlage legen für eine neue gerechtere internationale Ordnung, die global Hunger und Armut bekämpft [emphasis added] (Der Grüne Neue Gesellschaftsvertrag 2009:13).

Here, not only the beginning phrase is repeated, but also the first and the last sentences. This is done in order to create lexical cohesion and to wrap up the argumentation in a symmetrical manner, by starting in the first sentence with "[…] jetzt die Grundlagen dafür zu legen [...]" and ending in the last sentence by saying almost the same: "[...] jetzt die Grundlage legen [...]". The usage of these devices serve to state, not only that the sentence messages are all equally important to the Greens, but also to relate to the reader and to engage him in an appeal to *do* something. Therefore Beard's "moral value" point gains a foothold. The appeal towards the reader is a moral demand: aiming at the reader's belief to be *good* and to do good things. Important here is also to note that the Greens use the object form of the personal pronoun us = "uns". Here, one can either deduce that the Greens talk of themselves, meaning "It is the Greens who have to..." but more likely is that they – by saying "us" – mean the consolidated group of people, including the potential voter but definitely addressing the reader in an integrating gesture. Beard (2000: 24) calls this **"Pronoun reference"** and undermines this assumption by saying that: "'We' gives a sense of collectivity, of us all being in this together [...]".

---

[7] In the next citations, "Der Grüne Neue Gesellschaftsvertrag" will be abbreviated to DGNG

Metaphors

Beard (2000: 21) states that a "Metaphor is deeply embedded in the way we construct the world around us and the way that the world is constructed for us by others". This second part of the sentence is important when examining a political election manifesto which itself aims at persuading the reader of their ideology and therefore constructs in that sense the reader's world in regards to specific aspects. Striking examples of the Greens use of metaphors are the following that were found in the Green's manifesto. The first metaphor is *Finanzjongleur* (DGNG 2009:3, 29). That instead of saying (Finanz) makler, the Greens use the metaphor jongleur, animates the readers to associate from the compound word of "Finanz" and "jongleur" that the brokers in question figuratively juggle money, as if they were juggling balls, implying that they don't consider the money's (emotive) value. This is used to support the Greens political proposition. Apparently they intend to regulate the international financial markets by endorsing strong sanctions to increase the transparency of financial transactions (cf. 2009: 41-42). The next two metaphors also catch the reader's eye. They complement each other in an argument, and are even more important in regards to the essay's subject of analysis.

> Wenn der Einkaufskorb in Zukunft noch stärker strategisch genutzt wird, werden gierige Spritfresser und energieverschwenderische Klimakiller in den Haushalten immer weniger. [emphasis added] (DGNGV 2009:3, 124).

Both *Spritfresser* and *Klimakiller* belong to the metaphorical type of **personification**. Jones and Stilwell Peccei (2004: 46) say that the reason behind the politicians' usage of personification is that it "[...] entails giving human characteristics to inanimate objects or abstract ideas." *Spritfresser* for instance, gives human (or rather animal-) characteristics to the inanimate object of a vehicle. The term "fresser" is in German usually given in contexts of categorizing species into "Fleischfresser" or "Pflanzenfresser". Moreover is the verb "fressen" normally a reference to the way animals "eat". Next to that, the verb "fressen" also has a negative connotation when used as verbal assault to insult people as in 'Du *frisst* wie ein Schwein'. When the Greens therefore refer to a vehicle as a *Spritfresser*, the reader is motivated to think of a vehicle as a bad, animal- like object which gauges on fuel and that in inference acts as a *Klimakiller*, a destroyer of the climate. In reality of course, a vehicle can neither "fressen" (gauge) nor "kill" as in the term *Klimakiller*. This is a compound noun hybrid anglicism and stand as metaphor for the emotional aspect which the climate change topic has stirred in society.

Both phrases are "Green"- inflected terms that have derived from the current "climate change" discussion and that have established themselves within the discourse language regarding the topics of climate, co2 emissions and their result, the earth's greenhouse warming.

'The rule of three'

To complete this insight into the rhetorical world of the Greens within their election manifesto of 2009, a look will be cast at the structural device of political language called the 'rule of three' (cf. Jones/ Stilwell Peccei 2004: 49). Jones and Stilwell argue that humans around the world are aesthetically attracted, and have been attracted throughout history, to the use of "[...] things that are grouped in threes [...]". Known as cultural assets, the three kings, the Holy Trinity, and the three musketeers exemplify the obvious affinity towards groups of three. This fact has been taken up by politicians as a means to catch the listeners or readers attention and has developed into one of the most important techniques in political speech. The Greens use this device to group their cornerstones into an aesthetic, memorable bundle of three: "Unsere Koordinaten: ☐Klima – Gerechtigkeit – Freiheit". (DGNG 2009: 3,17). This example of the 'rule of three' contains slogan quality and structurally orientates itself towards other famous "three-part statement(s)" (Jones/ Stilwell Peccei 2004: 49) such as the famous call for "Liberté, Egalité, Fraternité" in the French Revolution (cf. 2004: 50).

3.1.3. Presuppositions

An example of a sentence in the "Der Grüne Neue Gesellschaftsvertrag" where the political means of presuppositions are used is the following:

> Es liegt an uns, dass wir unsere Gesellschaft gerechter machen und Blockaden wegräumen, die verhindern, dass jede und jeder eine echte Chance auf Teilhabe hat. (DGNG 2009: 13)

In this sentence at least two presuppositions are visible. The employment of the comparative adjective "gerechter" presupposes that society is currently not fair or not fair enough. The second presupposition is that they want to prevent, and therefore assume that "Blockaden" exist. In both cases, the reader will be brought to think about these issues that even though not addressed directly – still lure in the background as 'true' facts (cf. Jones/ Stilwell Peccei 2004: 42). Another very vivid example of a presupposition from the program can be seen in the sentence:

> Wir drängen auf internationale Abkommen, darauf, dass Steueroasen ausgetrocknet werden und die Spielhölle der Finanzjongleure geschlossen wird (DGNG 2009:29).

Here the adjective "ausgetrocknet" presupposes that the states (e.g. Switzerland or Liechtenstein) where people can deposit their wealth – metaphorically called "Steueroasen" – are *not* dried out and that the "Spielhölle" (metaphor) is the opposite of closed. On the contrary it implies that its "doors" are indeed wide open. This meaning which becomes only apparent when reading between the lines, serves as "background assumption[s]" (Jones/Stillwell Peccei 2004: 42). Just as they state, this presupposition that the Greens claim of Steueroasen and Spielhöllen is "taken for granted to be true regardless of whether the whole sentence is true" (Jones/Stillwell Peccei 2004: 42). The main point is to get the readers on board of the Green Party in order to receive their vote.

3.2. Anglicisms within the Green's Language

In the following analysis all relevant levels of linguistic analysis are analysed and ticked off in order to get a comprehensive insight in what kind of dimension the Greens performed "Sprachtransferprozesse" (Koll-Stobbe 2009: 22); the transfer of English linguistic material, into their vocabulary.

3.2.1. Levels of text composition. Location, Order and Frequency of Anglicisms

When reading through the manifesto with a special interest in borrowings, hybrids and pseudo loans several things attract notice. First of all: Almost all of the anglicisms that were used mainly appear in the headlines of the main chapters or subchapters. Only the most frequently used anglicisms such as *internet, job/s* and the differently assimilated versions of *fair* also appear in in the continuous texts. The lead anglicism of the manifesto is – no surprise – the borrowing 'internet'. More than 40 times, this term is used. On second place and third place the terms 'fair (-e,-er,-en,-ness)' and 'job/s' rank with both 37 matches. For the analysis of this study, only a certain number of anglicisms were extracted. These extracted words and phrases resemble three sorts of anglicisms: borrowings, hybrids and pseudo-anglicisms. The choice of extraction was random and followed no specific selection criteria, other than that most of the words or phrases were extracted because they had caught the eye due to their English features.

Table 1: Extracted Anglicisms and frequency of appearance

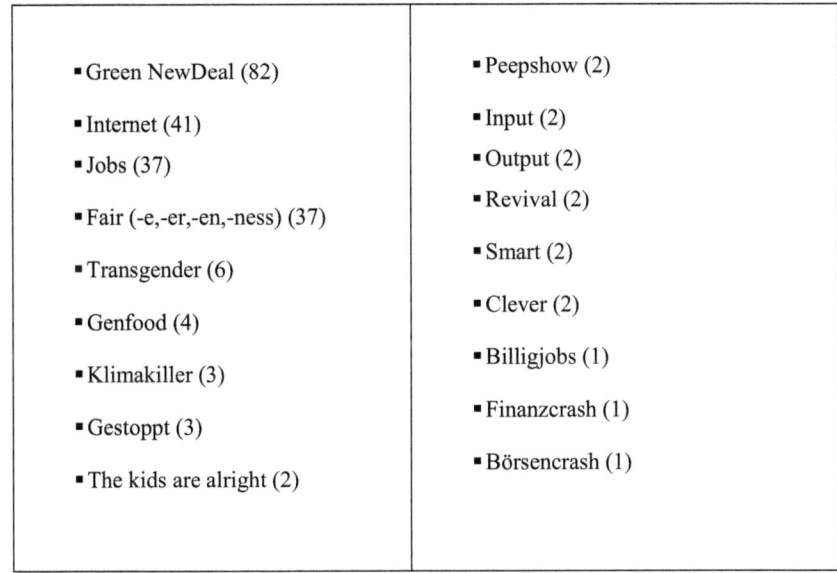

- Green NewDeal (82)
- Internet (41)
- Jobs (37)
- Fair (-e,-er,-en,-ness) (37)
- Transgender (6)
- Genfood (4)
- Klimakiller (3)
- Gestoppt (3)
- The kids are alright (2)
- Peepshow (2)
- Input (2)
- Output (2)
- Revival (2)
- Smart (2)
- Clever (2)
- Billigjobs (1)
- Finanzcrash (1)
- Börsencrash (1)

3.2.2. Lexical level: Borrowings, Hybrids and Pseudo- Anglicisms

When speaking of 'borrowings' in the study, also terms like loan and loanword are incorporated. These exist synonymously as result of the borrowing process. (cf. Onysko 2007: 11).

Borrowings

Direct loan influences found within the Greens program that have kept their original form are: *Internet, Revival, Jobs,* and *Peepshow.* These borrowings are only orthographically assimilated by the capitalisation of the first letter into the German language (cf. Koll-Stobbe 2009: 25). Nevertheless, both form and meaning from the SL, have been transferred into the RL. It can be moreover noticed that next to the fact that these borrowings don't change form on lexical level, they also don't particularly change on phonological level when transferred into German. This can however change, when speakers use a different pronunciation than the English standard to encode their local identity (cf. Koll-Stobbe 2009: 34). This would for instance be the case if a German speaker would say: Job: [tʃop], instead of GB/AE Job: [dʒɒb]. Filipović (cit. in Onysko 2007: 38/39) calls such a case "free transphonemisation" (cf.39). This is the case when the English sounds are unrestrictedly substituted by German sounds. (Onysko 2007: 39)

Furthermore, predicative adjectival anglicisms functioning attributively (cf. Onysko 2007: 254) like *clever, smart* and *fair* appear in the program. These adjectives occur as attributes to verbs and adjectives (cf. Onysko 2007: 254). In the Headline "clever und smart fürs Netz" (DGNG 2009: 6, 197), both adjectives refer to the Greens proposal for more skills in the area of IT-technology. For both borrowings: "clever" or "smart", no further explanation in German has to be given. Onysko in this regard argues that:

> [...] the adverbial use of adjectives and adjectival attribution are not morphologically marked [...], adjectival anglicisms are free from paradigmatic restrictions to specify the meanings of verbs and fellow adjectives. (Onysko 2007: 257)

But not only single word units are imported into the German text of the manifesto. Also multiple word unites are borrowed. Such a phrase from the manifesto is the main reference statement *Green New Deal*. A statement that derived from F.D. Roosevelt's "New Deal" which he proclaimed in the U.S.' economic crisis of the 1930's. Added is the supplement 'Green', marking the ecological orientation of economic policies. Not the German Greens coined this phrase, but the UNEP in their "Global Green New Deal" of 2008[8]. The second phrase which was borrowed, is the English sentence *The kids are alright* (DGNG 2009: 5, 118). This opens up a quite complex discussion because it reveals structural ambiguity on the level of presupposition. On the one hand one can see this simply as a kind of multi-word or phrasal anglicism to express a fact á la: "Den Kindern geht es gut". Referring to the passages of the chapter in which children/youths and care is the focus of attention. On the other hand, and this is more likely, the borrowed sentence phonetically sides with the movie title "The Kids Are All Right", an 2010 American 'feel-good' comedy-drama dealing with a lesbian married couple, their children and their children's donor. This assumption would fit especially because in the chapter before, the attention was primarily set on equal rights for homosexual couples. By using such a chapter heading, the authors expect from the reader to draw the connection to the movie on their own and to link the movie's message

---

[8] (http://www.unep.org/Documents.Multilingual/Default.asp?DocumentID=548&ArticleID=5957&l=en, DOA: 07.07.2012)

with the chapter's message. This presents a means of presupposition and is another reference to the extent with which the Greens tried to connect via language with their target group. A target group by the way that was so stirred by the movie that it now belongs to those films "one has to have seen".

Hybrids

Onysko (2007) states that "Hybrid anglicisms (hybrids) are based on a combination of English borrowings with German elements [...]" and that "Technically speaking, the inflection of anglicisms leads to a mixture of native and borrowed morphemes [...]" (cf.: 55). So clearly, we are confronted with a sign of language productivity in its makings. While using English lexemes and morphemes to combine them with German word units, the German lexicon is enlarged. Certain extracted nouns stand as samples to illustrate the Greens language. Koll-Stobbe (2009) argues that on lexical level these words stand as "[...] Prototyp dieser sprachlichen Identitätssignalsetzung zwischen lokaler und globaler/internationaler Kulturzugehörigkeit" (cf. 31). This is later elaborated on when she states that English is used as a means to transport its prestigious international culture, into the local language of culture which is German (cf. Koll- Stobbe 2009: 34). Therefore the emergence of hybrids like *Klimakiller, Billigjobs, Finanzcrash, and Börsencrash* can be explained from the line of argumentation Koll-Stobbe calls "Identitätsetzung" (2009: 34).

These "combinations of native and borrowed lexical elements" (Onysko 2007: 56), imply the Greens desire to internationalize their Argumentations – via Anglicisation – and appeal to their target group that has long since been internationally connected through social networks and currently almost standardised exchange programs.

Billigjobs, as one example of the extracted hybrids, is a German adjective + noun compound and belongs to the most frequently used hybrids. Onysko (2007: 193) calls this kind an: "endocentric (headed) compound(s)". It's semantic and grammatical part, here: *'Billig'*, stands at foremost position. *Jobs*, as the noun in this compound also belongs to the "Hitlist" of German borrowings. As a matter of fact the term *jobs* belongs next to *Filme* to the most frequently inflected forms. (cf. Onysko 2007: 118). The German suffixation -s marks the nouns plural form.

The semantic reason why a hybrid was used here can be deduced from the topic related context in which it stands. Here, the rhetorical use of a **contrastive pair** has been done. Within the preamble part it is stated that the Greens want: "[...] keine <u>Billigjobs</u>, sondern <u>Arbeitsplätze mit Zukunft</u>"(DGNG 2009: 14) [emphasis added]. *Billigobs* stand antithetically to work places that promise their employees a future ('Arbeitsplätze mit Zukunft'). Within the German language codex, the adjectiv *billig* is the vernacular, more negatively connotated synonym to *preisgünstig* or *günstig* and is used here - similar as in the case of *Sprit<i>fresser</i>*- to highlight the derogatory stance, the Greens hold towards the implication behind the label *Billigjob*. Or to be more precise: the Greens use this term to illustrate their adverse position towards the kind of job, where the employee hardly gets enough wage to compensate for his or her work.

Finanzcrash and *Börsencrash* are similar hybrids in terms of their structure. Both are endocentric compounds that carry their German part in front and their English noun in second position. The terms even mean on semantic level the same action of events, referring to the financial crisis that had started as 'subprime crisis' in the U.S. two years before. Here reasons behind using *crash,* instead of *-krise* might be the phonological effect of the onomatopoeic word *crash*. The German terms 'Finanz-' or 'Börsenkrise' have such a less dramatic sound quality - in comparison to the word-sound crash which in fact adds sound to the 'danger' radiating from its meaning.

c) Pseudo anglicims

The term *Genfood* consists of a compounded clipping of the English adjective 'genetically' (from 'genetically manipulated') and the lexeme 'food'. On semantic level the term refers to genetically manipulated food. On wordformation level however it presents a very interesting example of a pseudo anglicism. On the hand it is, just like Onysko (2007: 54) states, "[...] based on a novel combination and use of English lexical material [...]", on the other hand it differs in the way it should be pronounced in English. Other prime examples of pseudo anglicisms try to align themselves phonologically with the English pronunciation like *Dressman* or *Happy End*. Two terms that are pronounced (or at least tried to pronounced) the way an English native speaker would articulate the words. This is however not the case with *Genfood.* The first morphological unit *Gen* from *Genfood* is integrated into the German system of phonology and pronounced [gıən] (the sound /ıə/ as in ear and near) instead of [dʒen] from genetically: [dʒenetıkli:] (BrE/AmE). The second morphological unit, the free morpheme *food*, might also be assimilated to the German system of phonology but not in such a deliberate way as in the abbreviated bound morpheme *Gen*. Here the range between pronouncing it: [fu:d] (BrE/AmE) or very German inflected: [fʊ:t], depends on the individual speaker's skill or knowledge of the English pronunciation or their intention to mark their German (social) identity (cf. Koll-Stobbe 2009: 31). Why the Germans created the English inspired short term *Genfood*, despite the fact that in English speaking (L1) countries one simply says 'genetically modified food' or abbreviates it to 'GM foods' or 'biotech foods', can not be explained. It does however hint towards the fact that by using a compound word containing English elements, the Greens undertook (again) a step of "Identitätssetzung" (Koll-Stobbe 2009: 31) towards their intended international "Kulturzugehörigkeit" (31). On the one hand the term belongs to a set of established words from the German speaking field of Green discourse; on the other hand, this limited discourse zone strives to connect with its international, English speaking neighbour: the *international* Green language discourse community.

4. A Green Language?

Throughout the analysis many possible approaches were exposed attempting to define "Green Language". All approaches or strategies look at the motivation behind using anglicisms. For this study, the analysis of the motivational aspect seems to be the most logical step when the aim is to decipher how the Greens linguistically transported their messages through their manifesto.

There is however one flipside to the examination of anglicism motivation. Onysko (2004) argues in his article essay that the search for the motivation behind using anglicisms is of rather non-factual character:

> The most speculative and far-reaching answers concerning the phenomenon of Anglicisms in German revolve around the following question: Why are so many English borrowings integrated into German? (Onysko 2002: 62).

Nevertheless, for the result of this essay a clearly structured description of the three approaches towards the Green motifs to express their ideology embedded in a language studded with anglicisms, is essential. The two most convincing approaches that emerged are the concepts of: the emotive function of 'Modern Language' and the 'German Green field of discourse' and Identity.

The emotive function of 'Modern Language'

When examining the motivation behind using English language imports, the aspect of 'modern language' seems plausible. Since the atmosphere of 'modernity' and its implications are strongly connected with the way people feel, the notions stemming from the phrase 'something is modern' bear positive connotations and therefore carry an emotive function. Onysko quotes Fink and Augustyn who state: "Particularly in the language of advertisements, anglicisms are frequently used as emotional tools to create an atmosphere of modernity." (2007: 49). In addition, Onysko argues that:

> Today, English is an international voice that leaves its marks on the German language. Anglicisms in their original forms such as […] Internet, Homepage, Business […] are icons of the currents Zeitgeist in the German language (2007: 69).

When a party therefore wants to represent a certain kind of 'new politics', wants to address topics that are up-to-date, wants to attract a younger target group, then the use of anglicisms is the best way to accentuate the language of a speech or manifesto. Since it is now known that the topics the Greens are addressing likewise belong to 'Zeitgeist' issues and because it has been shown that the (aimed at) target group of the Greens is young, the motivation behind the Greens usage of anglicisms in their manifesto could plausible be explained with the aspect of 'modern language'.

The usage of *killer* in *Klimakiller* in the Green manifesto is a typical example for a stylistic motivation carrying emotive function. Onysko argues that:

> "English words are used as a means of variation, particularly in journalism, as with *Action* as a synonym for German *Handlung* and *Killer* for *Mörder*. *Team* is in complementary distribution with German *Mannschaft*, and in the case of *coach* and *Trainer* two Anglicisms allow for variation in German" (Onysko 2002: 62)

But also other metaphorical expressions (*Finanzjongleur, Steueroase*, etc.) are proof for the fact that the Greens' communication strategy is characterised by the use of vivid words and expressions in order to create variation and stylistic diversion and at the same time to trigger emotions that would not arise when using the German rather static equivalents.

Spitzmüller (2005) argues in his chapter on varieties and domains that certain restricted domains present individual language varieties consisting of a great number of borrowings. He outlines five domains which stand out in this context: The domains of business, advertising, mass media, IT and the leisure industries (cf. Spitzmüller 2005: 262). Even though political language – this study's subject of analysis – is not listed, the political manifesto of the Greens can still be seen as part of those domains. It seems convincing that just as product advertisings contain anglicised slogans, 'political language in a manifesto' is a variety that belongs the similar language code of advertisements. The study will thus see the language variety of 'political language in a manifesto' as belonging to the language variety of advertising.

To round off this assumption of 'modern language', the topic of 'language assimilation' needs to be mentioned. The Greens' target group consists in large parts of young, and well-educated Germans that provably make use of a vocabulary full of anglicisms. Koll-Stobbe even states that the younger German generation can be considered "funktional bilingual" (Koll-Stobbe 2009:29). A result of this is that the switch between German and English can be seen as a natural side effect (cf. Koll-Stobbe 2009: 31).

So the hypothesis would be: Just as young Germans tend to switch between German and English, the Greens, who want to assimilate in terms of language towards to their target group, use the same 'modern' idiolect of that speech community, using anglicisms in their language and therefore arousing emotions in their target group, who connects to the topics as well as to the language by which the often emotionally-charged topics are presented.

The 'German Green field of Discourse' and Identity

Metaphors, English borrowings, hybrids and pseudo-loans (e.g.: *Genfood*) that are concerned with the climate (e.g.: *Klimakiller*), stem from a discourse that has established itself in the last decade in Germany. Thus, by using terms that have originated from this discourse, the Greens promote their 'identity' and simultaneously secure their voters a value of recognition. These specific English words that have been used by the Greens within their manifesto could be therefore called 'cultural borrowings' or: "Kulturlehnwörter" (Koll-Stobbe 2009: 29). According to Koll-Stobbe, they derive from a certain field of language use or from "Sprachgebrauchskontext" (2009: 28).

In the case of the Greens, this field of language use would be the climate change discourse that has risen significantly in importance throughout the last decade. The globe encompassing movement of saving the environment has lead to an "own" discourse, with "own" words that are "Green inflected" and pitch up in many discussions that deal with climate change and its sub branches of discussion. Hence, metaphors like *Spritfresser* or *Klimakille*r portray prime examples of these topic bound compound words. They are signs of a "Green language".

Spitzmüller (2005) argues in his chapter on meta language discourses, identities and conflicts that in the second half of the 20th century, English as the language of the US that had acquired a leading role in economic, scientific and cultural terms, gained an immense social-symbolic "Mehrwert" (Spitzmüller 2005: 330). This 'added value' which the use of English implied, was then taken up by specific speech communities (cf. Spitzmüller 2005: 330). It can be argued that one of these specific speech communities is the group of speakers belonging to the Green discourse. Since this discourse has broadened its sphere of influence and has become an international issue also its language has internationalized itself, taking in words that stand for this sense of globe-encompassing fellowship amongst the Greens.

In the New York Times, an article on the German Greens stated this 'pioneer' character of the German Greens:

> The German Greens (also) have served as the spearhead of a global coming out for other Green parties. In Brazil's presidential election last year, the Green Party candidate won nearly 20 million votes to place third in the first round. The Green party in Colombia was founded just two years, ago but in 2010 saw its candidate for president place second. Britain's House of Commons welcomed its first Green Party member after last year's election, and Australia's Greens won their first seat in the lower house in 2002 (Kulish in: The New York Times 2011: A(4))

So when using anglicisms in their language, the Greens possibly want to mark their identity which means: being part of this international green discourse and at the same time use words that have established itself in this certain speech community around the topic of climate change.

Alternative Motifs

Of course many more approaches towards the motivation behind the usage of anglicisms have been made. Other possible reasons stated by Onysko (2002) are 'Semantic motivation (denotation)', 'Euphemistic' motivation, 'Social' motivation and the stylistic motivated usage of 'Conveniently short' anglicisms (cf. Onysko 2002: 62f.). With respect to the extracted anglicisms of the manifesto, the semantic motivation or denotation would for instance explain the usage of the term *Internet* (41 times throughout the paper). Onysko argues that:

> New products and inventions are frequently accompanied by their original English terminology, as with *Rollerblades, Internet, E-mail Account, Coffee-Shop, Computer*, and *TV-Soap*, to name a few. The denotative motivation is particularly dominating the lexical fields of special and technical languages: e.g. computer science, business, nuclear science (Onysko 2002: 62).

These other approaches are applicable and should therefore not be discharged when analysing the reasons behind anglicism usage. These approaches should be rather seen as 'complementing' each other because in most cases the motif is too complex than to be explained by only one motif.

5. Summary and Conclusion

The aim of this study has been to linguistically analyse the language of the German Green party. The focus was put on the language the Greens displayed in their manifesto to the parliament elections of 2009.

As stated in the introduction and throughout this study, the general question has been asking for a 'green language', meaning whether the Greens came up with a certain identifiable language, bearing an 'own code'.

My focus was set on the Greens and their manifesto because they represent a party that has gone through many changes in the last years and that has addressed topics that I can personally relate to considering myself as belonging to their 'target group' (see p. 8). Furthermore, I wanted to find out if the often negatively connoted aspect of anglicism usage would apply to the language of a German party. What better party then to look at, than the Green party who has always been keen on presenting its topics in a 'different' way?

In order to get a thorough insight into the Green party's language I provided the reader with a theoretical framework followed by a two-level empirical analysis.

Within the theoretical approach I argued that in order to grasp the Greens' language it is necessary to look at the Greens ideology, find out who their target group is and then examine their previous communication techniques. After this step had been conducted I moved to the different methods of political language. Since the Greens manifesto belongs to the variety of 'political language', it was important to see what kind of techniques politicians use in order to transfer their ideas. Here I concentrated on the three kinds of important rhetorical devices and the technique of presupposition, drawing on authors that dealt explicitly with political discourse analysis. After this rather brief insight to these devices and techniques, I worked my way up to give a theoretical approach to contact linguistics. Here I also used the strategy of deductive reasoning, so as to move from a broad topic, such as the historical background of 'German and English language contact', to the classification of anglicisms.

In chapter 3, I conducted the empirical analysis of the Green party's manifesto. First I described the election program on a surface level, giving an outline of its setup and its dimensions. Then I extracted certain phrases that I could match with a fitting technique of political rhetoric, be it metaphors or presuppositions – or both, and analysed them according to their composition, meaning and (when relevant) to their phonological quality. The same procedure I performed in the next chapter where I didn't look at discourse techniques but at contact-induced outcomes such as borrowings hybrids and pseudo-loans. In order to have a good overview over the words and phrases I had extracted from the manifesto, I created a table, listing up the anglicisms I had chosen to analyse and their frequency in which they appeared in the election program.

Throughout the rhetorical and linguistic analysis of the Greens language in the manifesto, the focus was always on the question *why* exactly these words had been used, with the attempt to resolve the rather broad and open question: 'Does a 'Green Language' exist?'

Looking at this question from a dual perspective I can answer in the affirmative that a 'Green language' exist. This answer is supported by the description of the two motifs the Greens have for using certain words. I subsumed these reasons for applying a certain language under the arguments of a)'the emotive function of 'Modern Language' and b) the 'German Green field of discourse' and Identity.

To a): Julian Scholl, the executive director of "Zum goldenen Hirschen," in charge for leading the Greens communication style in 2009, calls the Greens' language "moderne Sprache" [9]. Here I would come in arguing that what he calls 'modern language', I could call 'Green language'. The Greens draw on expressions (metaphors, hybrids, etc.) that exist in the already present canon of their target groups' variety not only to assimilate language-wise. They also transport their emotionally charged topics such as climate change in order to trigger emotions in this particular target group that would otherwise not respond emotionally to the rather static German equivalents for those expressions. It is, for instance, apparent that the terms '*spritverbrauchende und klimaschädliche Fahrzeuge*' would have a much less emotive expressiveness than: "gierige Spritfresser und energieverschwenderische Klimakiller" (DGNG 2009: 125).

---

[9] BÜNDNIS90/DIE GRÜNEN (2009): "Vorgestellt: Auffällig und kampfeslustig: Die grüne Wahlkampfagentur".In:*Mitgliederzeitschrift*.http://www.gruene-partei.de/cms/themen_mitgliederzeitschrift/dok/1/1322.vorgestellt.htm, DOA: 07.07.2012.

To b): The second strand of argumentation, stating that a 'Green language' exist, is what I call the 'German Green field of Discourse' and Identity. Hereby I argue that the Greens particularly use metaphors, English borrowings, hybrids and pseudo-loans that are connected to the climate change debate. These words mostly stem from a 'Green inspired' political discourse that established itself in the last decade in Germany revolving around the broad topic of climate change. Thus, by using terms that have originated from this discourse, an identity assignment takes place. The Greens set and promote a 'Green identity', constituting a certain variety that serves for a high recognition value for the target voters. This process could be called "Identitätssetzung" (Koll-Stobbe 2009: 34) and implies that together with a 'Green identity' also comes a 'Green language'.

However, this affirmative answer arguing that there is indeed a 'Green language' could be disputed. That is due to the reason that the rather limited scope of my study could not reveal that the Green party created a genuinely *own* 'green language' for its communication purposes. On the contrary, in its manifesto the Green party uses terms that already exist beyond the 'green' speech community. More specifically, the party uses certain words: metaphors, borrowings, hybrids or pseudo-loans that are common items in the 'tool-box' of the 'modern' language variety the younger German speech community draws on. Since this speech community belongs to the Greens' target group of voters it can be inferred that the Green party wants to, by means of its language, *only* assimilate to this 'trend variety' – this would imply they make use of a variety already existing, thus not displaying a 'Green language' of their own.

In order to find a precise answer to the question, a more comprehensive study would have to be executed. Not only one language example of the Greens would have to be looked at (as it was done in my study) – the linguistic analysis should also include campaign speeches of the Green party, campaign posters and analyse the Green Party's slogans. On that note I also suggest that further studies should focus on the normative discussion whether the usage of anglicisms by Green politicians – who do portray a language prescribing authority – is a rather downgrading move towards the German lexicon or if it actually serves for enriching the German language.

6. Bibliography

Primary Source:

BÜNDNIS90/DIE GRÜNEN (2009): "Bundestagswahlprogramm: Der Grüne Neue Gesellschaftsvertrag: Klima, Arbeit, Gerechtigkeit, Freiheit". Leck: CPI books. http://www.gruene-partei.de/cms/files/dokbin/295/295495. wahlprogramm_komplett_2009.pdf, DOA: 7.07.2012.

Secondary Sources:

Monographies

Beard, Adrian (2000): *The Language of Politics.* London: Routledge.

Carstensen, Broder/ Busse, Ulrich (1993): *Anglizismen-Wörterbuch: Der Einfluss des Englischen auf den deutschen Wortschatz nach 1945.* New York: de Gruyter.

Görlach, Manfred (2001): *A dictionary of European Anglicisms: A usage Dictionary of Anglicisms in sixteen European Languages.* New York: Oxford University Press.

Harms, Erik (2008): *Der kommunikative Stil der Grünen im historischen Wandel, Eine Überblicksdarstellung am Beispiel dreier Bundestagswahlprogramme.* Frankfurt am Main: Peter Lang.

Jenkins, Jennifer (2003): *World Englishes: a resource book for students.* New York: Routledge.

Locher Miriam A. (2004): *Power and politeness in action : disagreements in oral communication.* Berlin : Walter de Gruyter.

Onysko, Alexander (2007): *Anglicisms in German: borrowing, lexical productivity, and written codeswitching by Alexander Onysko.* Berlin: Walter de Gruyter.

Spitzmüller, Jürgen (2005): *Metasprachdiskurse: Einstellungen zu Anglizismen und ihre wissenschaftliche Rezeption.* Berlin: Walter de Gruyter.

Volmer, Ludger (2009): *Die Grünen Von der Protestbewegung zur etablierten Partei- Eine Bilanz.* München: C. Bertelsmann.

Edited volumes

Bolton, Kingsley/Kachru, Braj B., eds. (2006): *World Englishes. Critical Concepts in Linguistics.* Vol. 3. New York: Routledge.

Görlach, Manfred, ed. (2001): *English in Europe.* New York: Oxford University Press.

Heine, Bernd/ Kuteva, Tania (2005): *Language Contact and Grammatical Change.* Cambridge: Cambridge University Press.

Essays from an edited volume

Jones, Jason and Stilwell Peccei, Joan (2004): "Language and politics." In: Thomas, Linda/Wareing, Shan/Ishtla, Sing, et.al, eds: *Language, society and power/ an introduction.* USA: Routledge, 35- 54.

Koll-Stobbe, Amei (2009): "Anglizismen sind Bullshit: Entlehnungsprozesse und interkulturelle Identität." In: Koll-Stobbe, Amei, ed.: *Zwischen den Sprachen, zwischen den Kulturen Transfer- und Interferenzprozesse in europäischen Sprachen.* Frankfurt a. Main: Peter Lang Internationaler Verlag der Wissenschaften, 19- 42.

Journal essays

Winford, Donald (2007): "Some Issues in the Study of Language Contact". *Journal of Language Contact* (1): 22- 40.

Kulish, Nicholas (2011): "Greens Gain in Germany, And the World Takes Notice." *The New York Times*, Sept. 2, 2011, p. A4 (L).

Onysko, Alexander (2004): "Anglicisms in German: From iniquitous to ubiquitous?" *English Today*, Vol. 20: 59-64.

Onysko, Alexander (2009): Exploring discourse on globalizing English." *English Today*, Vol. 25 (1): 25-36.

Internet sources

Knospe, Sebastian (2010): "Ambiguisierende Nonce-Bildungen im deutsch-englischen Sprachkontakt – ☐ein Ausdruck von interlingualer Kreativität?" In: *Trans, Internet-Zeitung für Kulturwissenschaften.* Vol. 17: Section 5.6. http://www.inst.at/trans/17Nr/5-6/5-6_knospe17.htm, DOA: 07.07.2012.

BÜNDNIS90/DIE GRÜNEN (2009): "Vorgestellt: Auffällig und kampfeslustig: Die grüne Wahlkampfagentur". In: *Mitgliederzeitschrift.* http://www.gruene-partei.de/cms/themen_mitgliederzeitschrift/dok/1/1322.vorgestellt.htm, DOA: 07.07.2012.

Dietrich, Katrin/Keim, Nina (2006): "Die Wahlkampagne des Bündnis 90/Die Grünen zur Bundestagswahl 2005". http://www.fb9dv.uni-duisburg.de/wis/WIS5/Gruene/Medienarchiv/GrueneKampage.pdf, DOA: 07.07.2012

Deutscher Bundestag, Bundestagswahl 2009 (2009): "Das Endergebnis der Bundestagswahl 2009". http://www.bundestag.de/btg_wahl/index.html, DOA: 07.07.2012.